"REAL TIME HAND GESTURE RECOGNITION FOR MOUSE CONTROLLING FUNCTION"

MOUSE CONTROLLING FUNCTION

SUHAS BALIRAM KHADAKE

CHAPTER 1

Introduction

Hand gestures are an easy to use and natural way of interaction. Using hands as a device can help people communicate with computers in a more intuitive and natural way. When we interact with other people, our hand movements play an important role and the information they convey is very rich in many ways. We use our hands for pointing at a person or at an object, conveying information about space, shape and temporal characteristics. We constantly use our hands to interact with objects: move them, modify them, and transform them. In the same unconscious way, we gesticulate while speaking to communicate ideas ('stop', 'come closer', 'no', etc). Hand movements are thus a mean of non-verbal communication, ranging from simple actions (pointing at objects for example) to more complex ones (such as expressing feelings or communicating with others). In this sense, gestures are not only an ornament of spoken language, but are essential components of the language generation process itself [1].

The impendent of virtual environments brings in a whole new set of problems for user interfaces. The unveiling of 3D objects and worlds in which the user is engrossed allows such people as scientists, engineers, doctors and architects to envision composite structures and systems with eminent degrees of quality and naturalism. Shutter glasses furnish a stereo or 3D view of the scene, which is no longer confined to a desktop monitor, but may be a large table, projection screen or room. The limiting component in these systems currently is the fundamental interaction. Virtual environments seek to produce a world where the interaction experiences are real. Current mechanical, acoustic and magnetic input devices track the user and provide control of movement, selection and manipulation of objects in virtual scenes. Several tools are purported and used so far to make such interaction more and more prompt and effortless. Touch screens are the most widely used example: though the ramification of the underlying system is hidden from the user, and makes it possible for a user to point to the choices as he could do in real life. The cost associated to it is the major limitations of the aforesaid technology other limitations may be size, requirement of a physical location, and other intrinsic limitation to 2D [2].

In recent years applications like Human-computer interaction (HCI) and robot vision have been active research areas. The conventional Human Computer Interaction devices such as keyboard, mouse, joysticks, roller-balls, touch screens, and electronic pens, are inadequate for latest Virtual Environment (VE) applications. These devices restrict the complete utilization of high performance hardware due to their limited input characteristics. The VE applications offer the opportunity to integrate various latest technologies to provide a more immersive user experience. As compared to conventional HCI interface devices, the techniques using human body motions, speech, and eyeball movements provide more powerful and intuitive HCI interface. Human hands are frequently used for communication in our daily lives [2]. Hand gestures are the most natural and easy way of communication. This powerful and instinctive property of human hand makes them adequate as HCI devices. In the present work, different techniques for hand gesture recognition are effectively combined to perform a robust hand detection and gesture recognition. The main purpose of our implementation is to operate computer mouse actions by hand gestures using a low cost USB web camera. The computer mouse operations involve the motion of the cursor plus clicking operation. A method use existing technique of Haar-like feature based object detection, ROI hand gestures are recognized by using some algorithm [1]. Defining ROIs and searching within them significantly reduces computational time. An algorithm uses a set of Haar-like features, which processes a rectangular area of the image instead of a single pixel. To achieve real time performance, algorithm is used to automatically select the best features and build a cascaded classifier. Once gestures are recognized, and then they are assigned to different mouse events, such as right click, left clicks, undo, etc [5].

Gesture recognition can be seen as a way for computers to begin to understand human body language, thus building a richer bridge between machines and humans than primitive text user interfaces or even GUIs (graphical user interfaces), which still limit the majority of input to mouse. Reference used only the finger-tips to control the mouse cursor and click. His clicking method was based on image density, and required the user to hold the mouse cursor on the desired spot for a short period of time. A click of the mouse button was implemented by defining a screen such that a click occurred[11].

CHAPTER 2

Literature Survey

To improve the interaction in qualitative terms in dynamic environment it is desired that the means of interaction should be as ordinary and natural as possible. Gestures, especially expressed by hands have become a popular means of human computer interface now days [3]. Human hand gestures may be defined as a set of permutation generated by actions of the hand and arm [4]. These movements may include the simple action of pointing by finger to more complex ones that are used for communication among people. Thus the adoption of hand, particularly the palm and fingers as the means of input devices sufficiently lower the technological barrier in the interaction between the disinterested users and computer in the course of human computer interaction. Following are the research work studied and reviewed and below are some highlights about various researches in works.

1) X. Zhang, X. Chen, Y. Li, V. Lantz, K. Wang and J. Yang, "A framework for Hand Gesture Recognition Based on Accelerometer and EMG Sensors,", Man and Cybernetics- Part A: Systems and Humans, pp. 1-13, 2011.

This system shows hand gesture recognition method using both multichannel EMG and 3-D ACC signals. The processing of the two signal streams is carried out in the following steps.

1)Data Segmentation: The multichannel signals recorded in the process of the hand gesture actions which represent meaningful hand gestures are called active segments. The intelligent processing of hand gesture recognition needs to automatically determine the start and end points of active segments from continuous streams of input signals. The gesture data segmentation procedure is difficult due to movement epenthesis.

2) Feature extraction:Various kinds of features for the classification of the EMG have been considered in the literature. These features have included a variety of time domain, frequency-domain, and time–frequency-domain features. It has been shown that some successful applications can be achieved by time-domain parameters.

3) Tree-Structure Decision: A decision tree is a hierarchical tree structure consisting of a root node, internal nodes, and leaf nodes for classification based on a series of rules about the attributes of classes in non leaf nodes, where each leaf node denotes a class . The input sample data, including the value of different attributes, are initially put in the root node.

2) Conic, N., Cerseato, P., De Natale, F. G. B.," Natural Human- Machine Interface using an Interactive Virtual Blackboard", Image Processing, 2007. ICIP 2007. IEEE International Conference on (Volume: 5), pp.181-184.

In this system A two level approach to recognize hand gestures in real-time with a single web-camera as the input device. The low level of the approach is focused on the posture recognition with Haar-like features and the AdaBoost learning algorithm. The Haar-like features can effectively describe the hand posture pattern with the computation of "integral image". The AdaBoost learning algorithm can efficiently speed up the performance speed and construct a strong classifier by combining a sequence of weak classifiers. Based on the cascade classifiers, a parallel cascade structure is implemented to classify different hand postures. From the experiment results, we find this structure can achieve satisfactory real-time performance as well as very high classification accuracy For the high level hand gestures recognition, we proposed the context-free grammar to analyze the syntactic structure based on the detected postures.

3) R. Lienhart and J. Maydt, "An extended set of Haar-like features for rapid object detection," In Proceedings of ICIP02, pp. 900-903, 2002.

In this paper we introduce a novel set of rotated haar-like features, which significantly enrich this basic set of simple haar-like features and which can also be calculated very efficiently.

4) Nguyen Dang Binh, Enokida Shuichi, Toshiaki Ejima," Real-Time Hand Tracking and Gesture Recognition System", GVIP 05 Conference, 19-21 December 2005

In this paper, we introduce a hand gesture recognition system to recognize real time gesture in unconstrained environments. The system consists of three modules: real time hand tracking, training gesture and gesture recognition using pseudo two dimension hidden Markov models (P2-DHMMs). We have used a Kalman filter and hand blobs analysis for hand tracking to obtain motion descriptors and hand region.

The algorithm proposed in our recognition engine is

1. Choose initial search window size and location.

2. While hand is in view,

(a) Track and extract the hand from an image sequence.

(b) Verify the extracted hand region.

3. Using P2-DHMMs recognize the gesture, which gives maximum probability.

Hand detection in an image frame: *Extracting hand region.* Extracting hand based on skin color tracking [20], we drew on ideas from robust statistics and probability distributions with Kalman filter in order to find a fast, simple algorithm for basic tracking. Our system identifies image regions corresponding to human skin by binarizing the input image with a proper threshold value.

Finding a palm's center and hand roll calculation:In this method, the center of user's hand is given as first moments of the 2-D probability distribution during the course of hand tracking algorithm operation where (x, y) range over the search window, and I(x, y) is the pixel (probability) value at (x, y).

Hand tracking and measuring trajectories: We use Kalman filter to predict hand location in one image frame based on its location detected in the previous frame. Kalman filter is used to track the hand region centric in order to accelerate hand segmentation and choose correct skin region when multiple image regions are skin color.

Gesture Recognition: Hidden Markov Models are finite non-deterministic state machines, which have been successfully applied to numerous applications. They consist of fixed number states with associated output probability density functions (pdfs) as well as transition probabilities a_{ij}.

5) "New Hand Gesture Recognition Method for Mouse Operations", IEEE 2011.

In this paper, color is used as a robust feature to first define a Region of Interest (ROI). Then within this ROI, hand postures are detected by using Haar-like features and AdaBoost learning algorithm. The AdaBoost learning algorithm significantly speeds up the performance and constructs an accurate cascaded classifier by combining a sequence of weak classifiers.

The main purpose of our implementation is to operate a computer mouse action by recognizing hand gestures using a simple USB web camera. The system consists of two main modules,

1. Skin color based ROI extractor

2. Haar-like features based classifier

First, input image is converted from RGB to HSV color space. Next, ROI module segments the hand from background by using skin color. The minimum and maximum skin ranges are Hue = 0 - 20, Saturation = 30 - 150, and Value = 80 – 255. The skin color pixels, which have the values between these ranges, are selected. A rectangle is then drawn around the detected skin color area. This sub image is then fed to the Haar-like feature classifier.

Next, the Haar-like feature classifier detects and recognizes the subsequent gestures to be used for computer mouse operations. To meet the requirement of real-time performance, we train our classifiers with Haar-like features, which can be computed efficiently by using the integral image technique. We use a boosting algorithm which can efficiently get rid of false images and detect target images with selected Haar-like features stage by stage.

6) Paul Viola, Michael Jones, "Rapid Object Detection using a Boosted Cascade of Simple Features", accepted Conference on Computer Vision and Pattern Recognition 2001.

This paper describes a machine learning approach for visual object detection which is capable of processing images extremely rapidly and achieving high detection rates. This work is distinguished by three key contributions. The first is the introduction of a new image representation called the "Integral Image" which allows the features used by our detector to be computed very quickly. The second is a learning algorithm, based on AdaBoost, which selects a small number of critical visual features from a larger set and yields extremely efficient classifiers. The third contribution is a method for combining increasingly more complex classifiers in a "cascade" which allows background regions of the image to be quickly discarded while spending more computation on promising object-like regions.

7) Vladimir I. Pavlovic, Rajeev Sharma, and Thomas S. Huang, "Visual Interpretation of Hand Gestures for Human-Computer Interaction: A Review", IEEE Transactions on Pattern Analysis and Machine Intelligence, Vol. 19, NO. 7, July 1997.

The use of hand gestures provides an attractive alternative to cumbersome interface devices for human-computer interaction (HCI). In particular, visual interpretation of hand gestures can help in achieving the ease and naturalness desired for HCI. This has motivated a very active research area concerned with computer vision-based analysis and interpretation of hand gestures. We survey the literature on visual interpretation of hand gestures in the context of its role in HCI. This discussion is organized on the basis of the method used for modeling, analyzing, and recognizing gestures.

The goal is to estimate the parameters of the gesture model using measurements from the video images of a human operator engaged in HCI. Two generally sequential tasks are involved in the analysis. The first task involves "detecting" or extracting relevant image features from the raw image or image sequence. The second task uses these image features for computing the model parameters.

Feature Detection:

Feature detection stage is concerned with the detection of features which are used for the estimation of parameters of the chosen gestural model. In the detection process it is first necessary to localize the gesturer. Once the gesturer is localized, the desired set of features can be detected.

Gesture Recognition:

Gesture recognition is the phase in which the data analyzed from the visual images of gestures is recognized as a specific gesture. Analogously, using the notation, the trajectory in the model parameter space (obtained in the analysis stage) is classified as a member of some meaningful subset of that parameter space.

8) Wong Tai Man, Dr Sun Han Qiu, Dr Wong Kin Hong, "Thumb Stick: A Novel Virtual Hand Gesture Interface", 2005 IEEE International Workshop on Robots and Human Interactive Communication.

In this paper, we present a framework of video-based virtual hand input for using one hand called Thumb Stick, which consists of six key components in hand analysis & tracking – skin color segmentation, noise reduction, edge detection, connected component labeling, a contour line Condensation tracker with adaptive searching path, and thumb movement recognizer. This system not only allows user to use one hand to give input, but also provide five degrees of freedom.

In this propose the system architecture of hardware and software, and outline the key components of the framework in detail. The goal is to estimate the parameters of the gesture model using measurements from the video images of a human operator engaged in HCI.

Hardware and Software Framework:

In the design of hardware configuration, we try to figure out the basic or minimum requirement of wearable computing. This shows our proposed hardware and software architecture. In recent decades, the size of CCD camera, head-mounted display, and notebook become smaller and smaller, so we use these three devices as the basic architecture of system.

Skin Color Segmentation:

Segmentation is the subdivision of an image into components. Typically, segmentation leads to the separation of single objects from the background, thus implicitly producing a binary image in which each pixel is classified as pertaining either to the background or to the foreground (or, at least, to objects' edges).

Morphological Operators:

After skin color segmentation, some fragments are produced with the skin color region or in the background. These regions have a few pixels and may be assimilated to noise, which can be eliminated by the Morphological erosion operator. In the next step, Morphological dilation operator is applied to refine the remaining regions and construct a hand mask

Canny Edge Detection:

Canny edge detector is applied to the image because we use contour line as the measurement of the Condensation. J. Canny suggested in an efficient method for detecting edges. It takes grayscale image on input and returns bi-level image where non-zero pixels mark detected edges.

9) Qing Chen, Nicolas D. Georganas, Fellow, IEEE, and Emil M. Petriu, Fellow, "Hand Gesture Recognition Using Haar-Like Features and a Stochastic Context-Free Grammar", IEEE Transactions on Instrumentation and Measurement, VOL. 57, No. 8, August 2008.

This paper proposes a new approach to solve the problem of real-time vision-based hand gesture recognition with the combination of statistical and syntactic analyses. The fundamental idea is to divide the recognition problem into two levels according to the hierarchical property of hand gestures. The lower level of the approach implements the posture detection with a statistical method based on Haar-like features and the AdaBoost Learning algorithm. The higher level of the approach implements the hand gesture recognition using the syntactic analysis based on a stochastic context-free grammar.

Originally for the task of face tracking and detection, Viola and Jones proposed a statistical approach to handle the large variety of human faces. In their algorithm, the concept of "integral image" is used to compute a rich set of Haar-like features. Compared with other approaches, which must operate on multiple image scales, the integral image can achieve true scale invariance by eliminating the need to compute a multiscale image pyramid and significantly reduces the image processing time. Another technique that is used by this approach is the feature selection algorithm based on the AdaBoost learning algorithm. The Viola and Jones algorithm is approximately 15 times faster than any previous approaches while achieving accuracy that is equivalent to the best published results

10)Miss Sulochana M. Nadgeri, Dr. S. D. Sawarkar, Mr. A.D. Gawande, "Hand Gesture Recognition", Third International Conference on Emerging Engineering and Technology.

In this paper, an attempt to made to propose a system to recognize alphabet characters (A-Z) In real-time from color image sequence using "Continuous Adaptive Mean Shift Algorithm (CAMSHIFT)" tracking algorithm. The proposed system is based on three main stages: Skin color detection, hand tracking and hand gesture recognition. This system can successfully recognize hand gestures using CAMSHIFT algorithm.

11) Viraj Shinde, Tushar Bacchav, Jitendra Pawar, Mangesh Sanap, "Hand Gesture Recognition System Using Camera", International Journal of Engineering Research & Technology (IJERT), ISSN: 2278-0181, Vol. 3 Issue 1, January – 2014.

Most gesture recognition methods usually contain three major stages. The first stage is the object detection. The target of this stage is to detect hand objects in the digital images or videos. The system is consist of hand detection, hand gesture recognition and finger detection.

For this it uses camera as the input device, which captures the color image and the

depth map at 640*480 resolution. In order to segment the hand shape, we locate the hand position using the hand tracking function. Then, by thresholding from the hand position with a certain depth interval, a rough hand region can be obtained. For finger detection it uses two algorithm: 1) Near-Convex Decomposition 2) Thresholding decomposition

12) Ashwini M. Patil, Sneha U. Dudhane, Monika B. Gandhi, Nilesh J. Uke, "Cursor Control System Using Hand Gesture Recognition", International Journal of Advanced Research in Computer and Communication Engineering,Vol. 2, Issue 5, May 2013.

System architecture is an overview of hand gesture recognition and mouse control system. First the input image is converted to a binary image to separate hand from the background. Then centre of hand is calculated and computed calculated radius of the hand is found. Fingertip points are been calculated using the Convex Hull algorithm. All the mouse movements are controlled using the hand gesture.

Once we get an image from the camera, the image is converted to YCbCr from the color space RGB as shown in figure 1. Then, we define a range of colors as 'skin color' and convert these pixels to white; all other pixels are converted to black. Then, the centric of the dorsal region of the hand is computed. Once the hand is identified, we find the circle that best fits this region and multiply the radius of this circle by some value to obtain the maximum extent of a 'non-finger region'. From the binary image of the hand, we get vertices of the convex hull of each finger. From the vertex and canter distance, we obtain the positions of the active fingers. Then by extending any one vertex, we control the mouse movement.

CHAPTER 3

Problem Statement

This system is based on concept of Image processing. In recent year here is lot of research on gesture recognition using kinect sensor on using HD camera but camera and kinect sensors are more costly. This project is focus on reduce cost and improve robustness of the proposed system using simple web camera.

Hand gesture recognition, aims to design systems which can identify human hand gesture as an input and uses these gestures in order to control a device through mapping of command as an output. This system relies on camera, able to capturing video sequences by one or several camera to interpret and analyze the gesture. This system consists of four phases, Image acquisition, Pre-processing, feature extraction and classification.

Step 1: 1) There is need to design the system which will give highest accuracy in the field of computer vision technology by using Real-Time Hand Gesture Recognition.

Step 2: There are many techniques existing for the Real-Time Hand Gesture Recognition, but the accuracy & efficiency are the most important aspects to be considered in the field of Hand Gesture recognition. According to previous research this system is more efficient, accurate & reliable as compared to other.

Step 3: This Real-Time hand recognition system is three fold. 1) Hand detection, 2) feature extraction and 3) recognition. For recognition, various features with their own objectives are constructed from hand postures and compared according to the similarity measures and the Best- matched posture is used as a mouse action to control the cursor of the computer.

Step 4: This Proposed work is focus on reduce cost and improve robustness of the proposed system using simple web camera.

CHAPTER 4

Methodology

4.1 System Block Diagram of Hand Gesture Recognition:

Fig 4.1: Block Diagram of Hand Gesture Recognition

Generally there are three stages in most of the gesture recognition systems. The three stages may be enumerated as image pre –processing tracking and recognition stage as shown in Figure. In tracking, there are several researchers who have done the similar research like viola-Jones based cascade classifier, commonly used for face tracking in rapidly image processing. Cascade classifiers are currently considered more robust pattern detection against the noises and lighting conditions as well. For tracking Viola-Jones and several other researchers have developed algorithms used for face tracking in rapid image processing like HAAR cascade classifier. This is presently one of the robust detection techniques under different constraints like noise. Gesture as input of human computer interaction based applications is an emerging field in which many researchers have worked and proposed different practical techniques. Jain implemented a vision based hand gesture pose estimation based application for mobile devices. Pavlovic et al. accomplished in their work that the gestures of users must be explained logically for developing a good human computer interaction based system. Generally, pattern recognition methodologies are capable of solving the problem with humbler hardware and computation necessities. In the present research effort, we will consider these aspects by taking it as a reference to a smart interaction environment of virtual object manipulation and control. Here the user can execute different actions that translate into a command in an intelligent system and further execute the user requirements into practical actions.

4.2 Algorithm:

4.2.1 Hand Detection

In image acquisition phase system extracts the static background and sits idle till user puts his hand in front of the corresponding camera. Once the hand is placed in front of camera it detects the hand using haar like features.

- Haar like Feature

4.2.2 Preprocessing

Preprocessing is applied to images before we can extract features from hand images. Preprocessing consists of two steps:

1. Segmentation

- Segmentation is done to convert gray scale image into binary image.
- Otsu algorithm is used for segmentation purpose. In computer vision and image processing, Otsu's method is used to automatically perform histogram shape-based image thresholding, or, the reduction of a gray level image to a binary image.
- The algorithm assumes that the image to be threshold contains two classes of pixels or bi-modal histogram (e.g. foreground and background) then calculates the

Optimum threshold

1. Morphological filtering

In the morphological filtering, we apply a rule on the binary image. The value of any given pixel in the output image is obtained by allying set of rules on the neighbors in the input image.

- Dilation
- Erosion

4.2.3 Feature Extraction

In feature extraction, the edges of the segmented and morphologically filtered image are found. Canny edge detector algorithm is used to find the edges of the image. Then a contour tracking algorithm is applied to track the contour.

- Canny Edge Detector

The algorithm runs in 5 separate steps

1. Smoothing: Blurring of the image to remove noise.

2. Finding gradients: The edges should be marked where the gradients of the image has large magnitudes.

3. Non-maximum suppression: Only local maxima should be marked as edges.

4. Double thresholding: Potential edges are determined by thresholding.

5. Edge tracking by hysteresis: Final edges are determined by suppressing all edges that are not connected to a very certain (strong) edge.

4.2.4 Hand tracking:

The segmented hand from the input sequence is tracked in the subsequent phase. This is done by using modified CAMSHIFT based on the CAMSHIFT algorithm for hand tracking. CAMSHIFT is designed for dynamically changing distributions. This unique feature makes the system robust to track moving objects in video sequences, where size of the object and its location may change over time. In this way, dynamic adjustment of search window size is possible. CAMSHIFT is based on colors, thus it requires the availability of color histogram of the objects to be tracked the desired objects within the video sequences.

- Camshift Algoritm

4.2.5 Recognition

In the recognition phase the system extracts the features of the hand for gesture classification. The different gestures are differentiated by extracting features from the contours around hand and getting the convex hull of the given contour.

- NCN (nearest conflicting neighbors) Algorithm

CHAPTER 5

Hand Segmentation

Hand tracking and segmentation is the key of success towards any gesture recognition, due to challenges of vision based methods, such as varying lighting condition, complex background and skin color detection; variation in human skin color complexion required the robust development of algorithm for natural interface. Color is very powerful descriptor for object detection. So for the segmentation purpose color information was used, which is invariant to rotation and geometric variation of the hand [6]. Human perceives characteristics of color component such as brightness, saturation and hue component than the percentage of primary color red, green, and blue. Color models are useful for to specify a particular color in standard way. It is space-coordinated system within which any specified color represented by single point. Here, three techniques were introduced using different color spaces for robust hand detection and segmentation. Hand tracking and segmentation (HTS) technique using HSV color space is identified for the preprocessing of HGR system [6].

Hand segmentation is the pre-requisite to track the movement of the hand. There are various types of commonly used hand segmentation techniques as described below-

5.1 Hand Segmentation Techniques:

5.1.1 Background Subtraction:

In this technique, depending upon the skin color, the rest of the background is removed. By doing this, the hand and face parts are segmented as they have almost same color. After this, the face region in the frame is removed by using a face detection algorithm, since we are interested only on the hand motion. Then the original color plane is converted to two separate HSV and YCbCr color planes, and a threshold is applied to chrominance componentof both color spaces. RGB plane is converted to HSV because hue component gives the average of the R, G and B components. Saturation represents the amount to which that respective color is mixed with white and value represents the amount to which that respective color is mixed with black. A logical 'AND' operation is done between them to get the most probable skin region (hand). Noise is minimized using morphological operations like erosion, dilation etc [3]

Apart from the above two process, hand segmentation can be done with the help of background subtraction. In this method first, the image of our working background (without gesturer) is stored. Now the image frame (with gesturer) is subtracted from the previously stored background image plane. This gives the image of gesturer's body parts. Now we required to perform the operation for detecting face and segmented the moving hand. Disadvantage of this system is that if the lighting conditions change abruptly then there is a change in pixel value where the light intensity changed and additive noise contributes to the output [3]

The core of each motion detection system is the part of background subtraction that effectively extracts the correct shape of moving objects. In this paper, we have used the image Im of moving points detected by the temporal image analysis and the reference background image Bt evaluated at the time t. Radiometric similarity is used again for selecting from the moving points in Im those that are different from the model background image Bt. The resulting binary foreground image is obtained as follows [3]:

$$F^t(x, y) = \qquad \text{if } R(I_M(x, y), B^t(x, y)) < \acute{o}_s$$

5.1.2. Morphological Operation:

We cannot get a good estimate of the hand image because of background noise. To get a better estimate of the hand, we need to delete noisy pixels from the image. We use an image morphology algorithm that performs image erosion and image dilation to eliminate noise [1]. Erosion trims down the image area where the hand is not present and Dilation expands the area of the Image pixels which are not eroded. Mathematically, Erosion is given by [6],

$$A \ominus B = \{ \mid (B) x \cap A^c = \emptyset \}$$

Where A denotes input image and B denotes Structure elements. The Structure element is operated on the Image using a Sliding window and exact matches are marked Dilation is defined by [6],

$$A \ominus B = \{X \mid (\qquad) \cap A \neq \emptyset \}$$

$$= \{x \mid [(\qquad) X \cap A] \qquad A\}$$

Where A denotes the input image and B denotes the structure element. The same structure element is operated on the image and if the center pixel is matched, the whole area around that pixel is marked [6].

5.1.3 Haar Like Feature:

The simple Haar-like features (so called because they are computed similarly to the coefficients in the Haar wavelet transform) are used in the Viola and Jones algorithm. There are two motivations for the employment of the Haar-like features rather than raw pixel values. The first is that the Haar-like features can encode ad hoc domain knowledge, which is difficult to describe using a finite quantity of training data. Compared with raw pixels, the Haar-like features can efficiently reduce/increase the in-class/out-of-class variability, thus making the classification easier [3]. The Haar-like features describe the ratio between the dark and bright areas within a kernel. One typical example is that the eye region on the human face is darker than the cheek region, and one Haar-like feature can efficiently catch that characteristic. The second motivation is that a Haar-like feature-based system can operate much faster than a pixel based system. Besides the above advantages, the Haar-like features are also relatively robust to noise and lighting changes because they compute the gray-level difference between the white and black rectangles. The noise and lighting variations affect the pixel values on the whole feature area, and this influence can be counteracted. Each Haar-like feature consists of two or three connected "black" and "white" rectangles. Fig. 1 shows the extended Haar-like features set that was proposed by Lienhart and Maydt [1]. The value of a Haar-like feature is the difference between the sums of the pixel values in the black and white rectangles [3].

$$f(x) = \sum (\text{pixel value}) - \sum (\text{pixel value})$$

back back

A Haar-like feature considers adjacent rectangular regions at a specific location in a detection window, sums up the pixel intensities in each region and calculates the difference between these sums. This difference is then used to categorize subsections of an image. For example, let us say we have an image database with human faces. It is a common observation that among all faces the region of the eyes is darker than the region of the cheeks. Therefore a common haar feature for face detection is a set of two adjacent rectangles that lie above the eye and the cheek region. The position of these rectangles is defined relative to a detection window that acts like a bounding box to the target object (the face in this case) [1]. In the detection phase of the Viola–Jones object detection framework, a window of the target size is moved over the input image, and for each subsection of the image the Haar-like feature is calculated. This difference is then compared to a learned threshold that separates non-objects from objects. Because such a Haar-like feature is only a weak learner or classifier (its detection quality is slightly better than random guessing) a large number of Haar-like features are necessary to describe an object with sufficient accuracy. In the Viola–Jones object detection framework, the Haar-like features are therefore organized in something called a classifier cascade to form a strong learner or classifier [3].

Fig: 5.1.3.1 Extended set of Haar-like Feature

Fig: 5.1.3.2 Integral Image

The "integral image" at the location of pixel(x, y) contains the sum of the pixel values above and left of this pixel, which is inclusive

$$P(x, y) = \sum p(x', y')\ldots$$

$$x' \leq x, y' \leq y$$

According to the definition of the "integral image," the sum of the pixel values within the area *D* in Fig. can be computed by,

$$P_1+P_4-P_2-P_3$$

Where P_1=A, P_2=A+B, P_3=A+C, and P_4=A+B+C+D

To detect an object of interest, the image is scanned by a sub window containing a specific Haar-like feature based on each Haar-like feature *fj, a* correspondent weak classifier *hj*(x) is defined by

$$h_j(x) = \{ \qquad \text{if } p_j f_j(x) < p_j \Theta j$$

Where *x* is a sub window, and θ is a threshold. *pj* indicates the direction of the inequality sign. In practice, no single Haar-like feature can identify the object with high accuracy. However, it is not difficult to find one Haar-like feature-based classifier that has better accuracy than random guessing. The AdaBoost learning algorithm can considerably improve the overall accuracy, stage by stage, by using a linear combination of these individually weak classifiers [6]. It should be noted that a Haar-like feature could be repeatedly used in the linear combination. The AdaBoost learning algorithm initially assigns an equal weight to each training sample (see Fig. 4). We start with the selection of a Haar-like feature-based classifier for the first stage, retaining the first one that yields better than 50% classification accuracy. This classifier is added to the linear combination with strength that is proportional to the resulting accuracy. For the next stage, the training samples are reweighted; training samples that are missed by the previous classifier are "boosted" in importance. The next classification stage must achieve better accuracy for these misclassified training samples so that the error can be reduced. We retain the classifier that further improves the overall classification accuracy. The iteration goes on by adding new classifiers to the linear combination until the overall accuracy meets the required level. The final result is a strong classifier composed of a cascade of the selected classifiers [1].

5.1.4 AdaBoost learning algorithm:

In practice, no single Haar-like feature can identify the object with high accuracy. However, it is not difficult to find one Haar-like feature-based classifier that has better accuracy than random guessing. The AdaBoost learning algorithm can considerably improve the overall accuracy, stage by stage, by using a linear combination of these individually weak classifiers. It should be noted that a Haar-like feature could be repeatedly used in the linear combination. The AdaBoost learning algorithm initially assigns an equal weight to each training sample. We start with the selection of a Haar-like feature-based classifier for the first stage, retaining the first one that yields better than 50% classification accuracy. This classifier is added to the line combination with strength that is proportional to the resulting accuracy. For the next stage, the training samples are reweighted; training samples that are missed by the previous classifier are "boosted" in importance. The next classification stage must achieve better accuracy for these misclassified training samples so that the error can be reduced .We retain the classifier that further improves the overall classification accuracy. The iteration goes on by adding new classifiers to the linear combination until the overall accuracy meets the required level. The final result is a strong classifier composed of a cascade of the selected classifiers [2].

Fig: 5.1.4.1 Iteration of the AdaBoost learning algorithm

Fig:5.1.4.2 Detection of positive sub windows using the trained cascade

In practice no single Haar-like feature can detect the object with a very high accuracy. However, it is not difficult to achieve a series of weak classifiers with the accuracy slightly better than 50% using Haar-like features. The AdaBoost learning algorithm is a method to improve the accuracy based on a series of weak classifiers stage by stage [9]. The AdaBoost learning algorithm initially maintains a uniform distribution of weights over each training samples. In the first iteration, the algorithm trains a weak classifier using one Haar-like feature that achieves the best recognition performance for the training samples. In the second iteration, the training samples that were misclassified by the first weak classifier receive higher weights so that the newly selected Haar-like feature must focus more computation power towards these misclassified samples.

The iteration goes on and the final result is a cascade of linear combinations of the selected weak classifiers, i. e. a strong classifier, which achieves the required accuracy In practical implementation, the attentional cascade is employed to speed up the performance of the learning algorithm. In the first stage of the training process, the threshold of the weak classifier is adjusted low enough so that 100% of the target objects can be detected while keeping the false negative rate close to zero [10]. The trade-off of a low threshold is that a higher false positive detection rate will accompany. A positive result from the first classifier triggers the evaluation of a second classifier, which has also been adjusted to achieve very high detection rates[2].

5.2 Architecture Design For Hand Detection:

Camera

Color the region to black

Color the region to white

If average pixel value > threshold

Diamond: If average pixel value >
threshold

Scan image with kernal of 4x4 and calculate average pixel value

Hand Detected

Store the current location and calculate pixel average value at given location

Locate had using stored xml file

Store Background

Background Subtaction

NO Yes

Get the segmented area of Hand

Fig 5.2 Architecture Design For Hand Detection

In the current system, during the image acquisition phase system extracts the static background and sits idle till user puts his hand in front of the corresponding camera as shown in figure 2. Once the hand is placed in front of camera it detects the hand using haar like features. A haar cascade xml is created for detection of hand. The haar-like characteristics are comparatively robust to the noise and lighting changes as the features will compute the gray level difference between the black and the white rectangles. The noise and lighting variations also strike the pixel measures on the entire characteristic region, which could be counteracted [5].

The reason for this strategy is based on the fact that the majority of the sub-windows are negative within a single image frame, and it is a rare event for a positive sub-window to go through all of the stages. With this strategy, the cascade can significantly speed up the processing time as the initial weak classifiers try to reject as many negative sub-windows as possible and more computation power will be focused on the more difficult sub-windows that passed the scrutiny of the initial stages of the cascade. In our implementation, four hand postures are tested: the two-finger posture, the palm posture, the fists posture and the little finger posture. The camera used for the video input in our experiment is a low-cost Logitech QuickCam web-camera that provides video capture with the resolution of 320x240, 15 frames-per-second.

Segmentation is the subdivision of an image into components. Typically, segmentation leads to the separation of single objects from the background, thus implicitly producing a binary image in which each pixel is classified as pertaining either to the background or to the foreground (or, at least, to objects' edges). Consequently, pixels of binary images can only be one of the two colors, typically black and white. Segmentation can be performed in the color domain as well, by searching for the image areas which have similar chromatic characteristics. For example, we will see the (skin) color-based segmentation is very often used to separate the face or the hands from the background, typically for hand tracking or gesture recognition[8].

CHAPTER 6

Hand Tracking

6.1 Camshift Algorithm:

The Camshift algorithm is based on the Mean Shift algorithm. The Mean Shift algorithm works well on static probability distributions but not on dynamic ones as in a movie. Camshift is based principles of the Mean Shift but also a facet to account for these dynamically changing distributions. Camshift's is able to handle dynamic distributions by readjusting the search window size for the next frame based on the zeroth moment of the current frames distribution. This allows the algorithm to anticipate object movement to quickly track the object in the next scene. Even during quick movements of an object, Camshift is still able to correctly track. The Camshift algorithm is a variation of the Mean Shift algorithm.Camshift works by tracking the hue of an object, in this case, flesh color. The movie frames were all converted to HSV space before individual analysis [4].

CAMSHIFT was implemented as such:

1. Initial location of the 2D search window was computed.
2. The color probability distribution is calculated for a region slightly bigger than the mean shift search window.
3. Mean shift is performed on the area until suitable convergence. The zeroth moment and centroid coordinates are computed and stored.
4. The search window for the next frame is centered around the centroid and the size is scaled by a function of the zeroth movement.
5. Go to step 2.

The initial search window was determined by inspection. Adobe Photoshop was used to determine its location and size. The initial window size was just big enough to fit most of the hand inside of it. A window size too big may fool the tracker into tracking another flesh colored object. A window too small will mostly quickly expand to an object of constant hue, however, for quick motion, the tracker may lock on the object or the background. For this reason, a hue threshold should be utilized to help ensure the object is properly tracked, and in the event that an object with mean hue not of the correctly color is being tracked, some operation can be performed to correct the error. For each frame, its hue information was extracted. We noted that the hue of human flesh has a high angle value. This simplified our tracking algorithm as the probability that a pixel belonged to the hand decreased as its hue angle did. Hue thresholding was also performed to help filter out the background make the flesh color more prominent in the distributions. The zeroth moment, moment for x, and moment for y were all calculated. The centroid was then calculated from these values [4].

xc = M10 / M00; yc = M01 / M00............................6.1.1

The search window was then shifted to center the centroid and the mean shift computed again. The convergence threshold used was T=1. This ensured that we got a good track on each of the frames. A 5 pixel expansion in each direction of the search window was done to help track movement. Once the convergent values were computed for mean and centroid, we computed the new window size. The window size was based on the area of the probability distribution. The scaling factor used was calculated by:

s = 1.1 * sqrt(M00)...6.1.2

The 1.1 factor was chosen after experimentation. A desirable factor is one that does not blow up the window size too quickly, or shrink it too quickly. Since the distribution is 2D, we use the sqrt of M00 to get the proper length in a 1D direction. The new window size was computed with this scaling factor. It was noted that the width of the hand object was 1.2 times greater than the height. This was noted and the new window size was computed as such:

W = [(s) (1.2*s)]...6.1.3

The Camshift algorithm is a variation of the Mean Shift algorithm.Camshift works by tracking the hue of an object, in this case, flesh color. The movie frames were all converted to HSV space before individual analysis. Camshift's is able to handle dynamic distributions by readjusting the search window size for the next frame based on the zeroth moment of the current frames distribution[4].

6.2Architecture Design For Hand Tracking:

Divide the image into four regions (R_1, R_2, R_3, R_4)

Calculate the number of white pixel in each region

P_1- No. of white pixel in R_1 / Total pixels in R_1

P_1- No. of white pixel in R_2 / Total pixels in R_2

P_1- No. of white pixel in R_4 / Total pixels in R_4

P_1- No. of white pixel in R_3 / Total pixels in R_3

$(P_1 + P_4)$

$>$

(P_2+P_3)

Move Right

Move Left

$(P_1 + P_4)$

$>$

(P_2+P_3)

Move Up

Move Down

Get the segmented region of the hand

Fig 6.2 Architecture Design For Hand Tracking

The segmented hand from the input sequence is tracked in the subsequent phase. This is done by using modified CAMSHIFT based on the CAMSHIFT algorithm for hand tracking. CAMSHIFT is designed for dynamically changing distributions. This unique feature makes the system robust to track moving objects in video sequences, where size of the object and its location may change over time. In this way, dynamic adjustment of search window size is possible. CAMSHIFT is based on colors, thus it requires the availability of color histogram of the objects to be tracked the desired objects within the video sequences. As mentioned earlier, the color model was built in the HSV domain on the basis of the hue component[1]. The spatial mean value is computed by selecting the size and initial position of the search window. The search window is moved towards center of the image in subsequent steps. Once the search window is centered computing is done through the centroid with first-order instant for x, y. The process is continued till it arrived at the point of convergence. In the implemented tracking process the image is divided into four regions R1, R2, R3, and R4. Then the number of white pixels in each of the four divided regions is calculated based on the total number of pixels. In order to find the position of hand in the divided regions we calculate p1, p2, p3, p4 the position values of hand tracked in the corresponding region. The position values are calculated using the equations as shown in figure the calculated position values are then added and compared for their respective regions to track the movement of hand. Based on the position values calculated and hand movement thus tracked is in turn mapped with the commands in the specific application [1].

The segmented hand from the input sequence is tracked in the subsequent phase. This is done by using modified CAMSHIFT based on the CAMSHIFT algorithm for hand tracking. CAMSHIFT is designed for dynamically changing distributions. This unique feature makes the system robust to track moving objects in video sequences, where size of the object and its location may change over time. In this way, dynamic adjustment of search window size is possible. CAMSHIFT is based on colors, thus it requires the availability of color histogram of the objects to be tracked the desired objects within the video sequences. As mentioned earlier, the color model was built in the HSV domain on the basis of the hue component. The spatial mean value is computed by selecting the size and initial position of the search window.

CHAPTER 7

Recognition

7.1 Architecture Design For Recognition:

Merge all the conflicting features

Find the convex hull of this contour

Extract the biggest (area) contour from the image

Find Contours around the image

Set region of interest (ROI) of image

Get Segmented Image

Count no. of defects

Find orientation of the bounded region

Get the direction of the image from the movement of the tracking region

Store all the information in the feature list

Confli CHAPTER 8

Iterative Update rule

cting O/P

Diamond: Confli CHAPTER 8 Iterative
Update rule cting O/P YES

No

Map the gesture value to generate a command

Fig 7.1 Architecture Design For Recognition

In the recognition phase as shown in figure the system extracts the features of the hand for gesture classification. In the recognition phase the system extracts the features of the hand for gesture classification. The different gestures are differentiated by extracting features from the contours around hand and getting the convex hull of the given contour. One can identify different gestures by counting the numbers of defects in the convex hull and it is relative orientation in its bounding rectangle. The features are classified into 8 classes, which are classified by a widely used algorithm for recognition called NCN (nearest conflicting neighbors).The recognition phase of the proposed two hand gesture recognition system takes the segmented image as input. The region of interest in the segmented image is identified and set first. Then the system finds the contour around the image and biggest area around the contour of the image is extracted to find the convex hull of this contour. Once the convex hull s found the number of defects in the image is calculated and orientation of the bonded region of image is found. Next the direction of the image is taken from the movement of the tracking region [1].

7.2: Concept of Contours, Convex Hull and Centroid:

7.2.1 Contours:

Fig 7.2.1 Contour

Parameters:

Centroid:-The centroid (px, py) of the blob (hand)

Angle:-The orientation/angle made by the blob (hand) with the horizontal.

7.2.2 Convex Hull:

Fig 7.2.2 Convex Hull

The convex hull or convex envelope of a set *X* of points in the Euclidean plane or Euclidean spaceis the smallest convex set that contains X. For instance, when *X* is a bounded subset of the plane, the convex hull may be visualized as the shape formed by a rubber band stretched around X.Formally, the convex hull may be defined as the intersection of all convex sets containing *X* or as the set of all convex combinations of points in X. With the latter definition, convex hulls may be extended from Euclidean spaces to arbitrary real vector spaces; they may also be generalized further, to [5].

7.2.3 Centroid:

we can calculate the center of the hand with the following equation:

Where i x and i y are x and y coordinates of the pixel in the hand region, and k denotes the number of pixels in the region. After we locate the center of the hand, we compute the radius of the palm region to get hand size. To obtain the size of the hand, we draw a circle increasing the radius of the circle from the center coordinate until the circle meets the first black pixel. When the algorithm finds the first black pixel then it returns to the current radius value. This algorithm assumes that when the circle meets the first black pixel, after drawing a larger and larger circle, then the length from the center is the radius of the back of the hand. Thus, the image segmentation is the most significant part because if some of the black pixels are made by shadows and illuminations near the center, then the tracking algorithm will meet earlier than the real background and the size of the hand region becomes smaller than the real hand [5].

Once the convex hull s found the number of defects in the image is calculated and orientation of the bonded region of image is found. Next the direction of the image is taken from the movement of the tracking region. All this collected information is stored in the features list. Next all the conflicting features in the feature list are merged if there are more conflicting features then they are merged again if no conflicting features remain in the feature list then the gesture value is mapped to generate the corresponding command. In the recognition phase the system extracts the features of the hand for gesture classification. The different gestures are differentiated by extracting features from the contours around hand and getting the convex hull of the given contour.

The task of optimal partitioning is usually addressed through different earning-from examplestraining procedures. The key concern in the implementation of the recognition

procedure is computational efficiency. We discuss each of the above issues in more detail. The task of optimal partitioning of the model parameter space is related to the choice of the gestural models and their parameters, as mentioned in Section 2. However, most of the gestural models are not implicitly designed with the recognition process in mind.

This is especially true for the models of static gestures or hand postures. For example, most of the static models are meant to accurately describe the visual appearance of the gesturer's hand as they appear to a human observer. To perform recognition of those gestures, some type of parameter clustering technique stemming from vector quantization (VQ) is usually used. Briefly, in vector quantization, an *n*-dimensional space is partitioned into convex sets using *n*-dimensional hyperplanes, based on training examples and some metric for determining the nearest neighbor. If the parameters of the model are chosen especially to help with the recognition, as for example in the separation of classes belonging to different gestures can be done easily.However, if the model parameters are not chosen to properly describe the desired classes, the separation of the classes, and thus, accurate recognition in that parameter space may not be possible. For example, with contour descriptors, several hand postures would be confused during classification and recognition [7].

CHAPTER 8

Result Analysis

8.1Red colour cap-Mouse Pointer

Step 1: Mouse Pointer movement can be done using red colour cap

Fig 8.1.1:Mouse Pointer with red colour cap

Step 2: With the help of mouse pointer with red colour cap one folder is choosen

Fig 8.1.2: Mouse pointer Function

8.2 One blue cap-Left click

Step 3: Left click function can be done using single blue colour cap

Fig 8.2.1:Red colour cap and single blue colour cap

Step 4: With the help of mouse pointer with red colour cap and single one blue colour cap folder is selected.

Fig 8.2.2:Left click function

8.3 Two Blue Cap-Right click

Step 5:Right click function can be done using Two blue colour cap

Fig 8.3.1: Red colour cap and single blue colour cap

Step 6: With the help of mouse pointer with red colour cap and two blue colour cap folder is open.

Fig 8.3.2: Right click function

8.4 Three Blue caps-Double click

Step 7: Doubble click function can be done using Three blue colour cap

Fig 8.4.1:Red colour cap and three blue colour cap

Step 8: With the help of mouse pointer with red colour cap and three blue colour cap folder is opened.

Fig 8.4.2: Doubble click function

8.5 Green Colour cap-Scrolling

Step 9: Scrolling function can be done using Green colour cap

Fig 8.5.1: Red colour cap and green colour cap

Step 10: With the help of mouse pointer with red colour cap and With the help of Green colour cap scrolling function is performed.

Fig 8.5.2: Scrolling function

CHAPTER10

Conclusions

Gesture based interfaces allow human computer interaction to be in a natural as well as intuitive manner. It makes the interaction device free which makes it useful for dynamic environment It is though unfortunate that with the ever increasing interaction in dynamic environments and corresponding input technologies still not many applications are available which are controlled using current and smart facility of providing input which is by hand gesture. The most important advantage of the usage of hand gesture based input modes is that using this method the users get that ability to interact with the application from a distance without any physical interaction with the keyboard or mouse.

A hand gesture recognition system which is used for browsing images in the image browser and provides a fruitful solution towards a user friendly interface between human and computer using and gestures. For optimized hand gesture recognition, in this paper, we have combined existing recognition techniques of skin color based ROI segmentation and Viola-Jones object detection. The recognized gestures are used as commands for mouse operation actions.

Future Scope

- Hand gestures are used to control various applications like windows media player, robot control, gaming etc.
- The complete computer system could be then operated with the help of human gesture we can also integrate the human voice

command for computing operations to be performed. This then would turn the phase of human computing.

References

1. X. Zhang, X. Chen, Y. Li, V. Lantz, K. Wang and J. Yang, "A framework for Hand Gesture Recognition Based on Accelerometer and EMG Sensors,", Man and Cybernetics- Part A: Systems and Humans, pp. 1-13, 2011.
2. Conic, N., Cerseato, P., De Natale, F. G. B.,: Natural Human- Machine Interface using an Interactive Virtual Blackboard, In Proceeding of ICIP 2007, pp.181-184, (2007) pdf.
3. R. Lienhart and J. Maydt, "An extended set of Haar-like features for rapid object detection," In Proceedings of ICIP02, pp. 900-903, 2002.
4. Nguyen Dang Binh, Enokida Shuichi, Toshiaki Ejima, "Real-Time Hand Tracking and Gesture Recognition System", 2005.
5. Ehsan ul haql, Syed Jahanzeb Hussain Pirzadcl, Mirza Waqar Bailand Hyunchul Shin, "New Hand Gesture Recognition Method for Mouse Operations", IEEE 2011.
6. Paul Viola, Michael Jones, "Rapid Object Detection using a Boosted Cascade of Simple Features", accepted Conference on Computer Vision and Pattern Recognition 2001.
7. Vladimir I. Pavlovic, Rajeev Sharma, and Thomas S. Huang, "Visual Interpretation of Hand Gestures for Human-Computer Interaction: A Review", IEEE Transactions on Pattern Analysis and Machine Intelligence, Vol. 19, NO. 7, July 1997.
8. Wong Tai Man, Dr Sun Han Qiu, Dr Wong Kin Hong, "Thumb Stick: A Novel Virtual Hand Gesture Interface", 2005 IEEE International Workshop on Robots and Human Interactive Communication.
9. Qing Chen, Nicolas D. Georganas, Fellow, IEEE, and Emil M. Petriu, Fellow, "Hand Gesture Recognition Using Haar-Like Features and a Stochastic Context-Free Grammar", IEEE Transactions on Instrumentation and Measurement, VOL. 57, No. 8, August 2008.
10. Miss Sulochana M. Nadgeri, Dr. S. D. Sawarkar, Mr. A.D. Gawande, "Hand Gesture Recognition", Third International Conference on Emerging Engineering and Technology.
11. Viraj Shinde, Tushar Bacchav, Jitendra Pawar, Mangesh Sanap, "Hand Gesture Recognition System Using Camera",International Journal of Engineerin Research & Technology (IJERT), ISSN: 2278-0181, Vol. 3 Issue 1, January-2014.
12. Ashwini M. Patil, Sneha U. Dudhane, Monika B. Gandhi, Nilesh J. Uke, "Cursor Control System Using Hand Gesture Recognition", International Journal of Advanced Research in Computer and Communication Engineering,Vol. 2, Issue 5,May-2013

Annexture

Publication of Paper

Sr. No

Title of paper

International/ National Journal or Conference

Date

1.

Real-Time Hand Gesture Recognition for Mouse Controlling Function

International Conference of Advances in Engineering sciences & Technology ICAEST-2016

6th-7th Feb 2016

2.

Real-Time Hand Gesture Recognition System

International Journal of Research Publications

In Engineering & Technology IJRPET-2016

February-2016

Contents

Printed by Libri Plureos GmbH in Hamburg,
Germany